PASSING IT ON

before

PASSING ON

Insights on Healing

from Interpersonal Trauma and Addictions

H. L. Foster, M.Ed.

Cover Design: Diane Tibert & H.L. Foster

Interior Design by Rik: Wild Seas Formatting

Edited by Diane Tibert

Paperback ISBN: 978-1-7753055-1-4

Electronic ISBN: 978-1-7753055-0-7

Dedication

In order of appearance in my life, I dedicate this sharing to:

Friends: Ruth, Dorice, Suzanne, Monique, Marlene, LaRue

Sons: Greg and Dave

Daughter-in-law: Angela

Granddaughters: Nadia and Leah

THANK YOU

CONTENTS

Author's Note

I believe my true Nature is Creative Energy, born into the form of me.

I believe fear and traumatic experiences made connection to my body too uncomfortable, so I moved into an overthinking mind. This dissociation grew a self-image that crowded out most signals from my true Nature.

I used alcohol to numb the pain of this disconnect.

Recovery had to begin with reconnection to my body. Only when I felt safe enough and supported enough could I drop down from my head. This began to happen for me in Twelve-step meetings.

While sharing, I began to discern my true Nature coming through SOME of the time; most often, I heard the dissociated ego parroting conditioned thought.

A vertical reunion with my internal signals is leading me into a new horizontal relationship with the world of appearances.

While my true Nature is reclaiming its rightful place, the rogue ego's self-image is experiencing an undoing in order to re-align with and serve my true Nature.

Since a virtual coup is taking place, it's no wonder both mind and body feel internal earthquake tremors.

The courage to stay with this unsettling process has been supported by others who shared their own experiences of re-alignment.

Terminology Used

self: ego, personality, self-image, i

Self (Dr. Carl Jung's term): True Nature, Centre, soul

Creative Energy: Source of Power, It, God, greater than ego

Egoic mind: dissociated self, overthinking mind, attempting to control Life mind. (Reference Ed Harris in *The Truman Show* movie)

reality: ego projection and reflection, ego illusion of horizontal cause and effect

insanity: reaction to *appearances*, unaware of their egoic origin

*REAL*ity: flashes of intuition and inspiration piercing commonly agreed upon *reality*. (Reference *The Truman Show* movie)

Introduction

Recently retired from private practice as a professional counsellor, workshop leader, teacher, and group facilitator, I have had life experiences many can relate to: only child, early childhood sexual abuse, eating disorder, cancer survivor, domestic abuse and violence, divorce, alcoholism, diagnosis of clinical depression, and hospitalization to confirm manic depression following the traumatic deaths of both parents in a car accident.

Despite my seeking professional help, trauma was never given a name or addressed.

I self-medicated with alcohol in an attempt to regulate what early trauma had physically and emotionally dysregulated before the psychiatrist prescribed medication.

I didn't know how to live in my own skin physically or emotionally around people; only animals and nature could be trusted for comfort.

Although attempted several times, a close intimate relationship was unsustainable.

There had been much remorse, regret, guilt, shame, and confusion around this inability as I relentlessly sought healing and answers.

An anonymous Twelve-step Program and trauma treatment are credited with resolving a great deal. Realizing in groups that I was not alone, helped lift and soothe what had been so personalized and isolating.

What remains, I no longer pathologize; it's an integral part of my human experience, not to be hidden in shame or escaped from.

I am excited to share what life was like, what happened during healing, and what life is like now.

I will begin with what life was like, followed by the *story* of me.

Then I will reveal how trauma, coincidences, and intuitive flashes informed my understanding of addictions and a way back to living my true Nature.

PART I

WHAT LIFE WAS LIKE

My true Nature was born into this physical life knowing a connectedness to All that is. I felt curious and excited, blissfully unaware of any need for safety or trust.

As an only child, sitting on the beach at our summer cottage, I talked to the lake and striped chipmunks while painting faces on little acorns wearing French berets. Connected, I felt a *yummy in the tummy* feeling.

Winter came and my best friend showed me her baby sister's grave, marked by a little white cross outside the Catholic graveyard. She explained that her baby sister couldn't go to Heaven because she hadn't received *The Last Rights*. I knew this couldn't be.

With spring, came Easter weekend, and a car drove through our circular driveway, killing my black and white kitty. This cat was my only sibling and I knew we would see each other again in Heaven. Sixty-five years later, the reigning Pope said he believed pets and animals do go to Heaven. I didn't need this affirmed.

As a child, I just knew things; that is, until I heard labels that seemed to mean *other than*.

This happened when two little children appeared one day on the beach property next to ours. I felt curious until mother said they were renters; then I felt confused and afraid. What were *renters*?

When my new kitty wandered across their property and into the bushes, I feared they wouldn't allow me to get her. I'd need a plan. After much anguish, I came up with the idea of inviting the two neighbourhood children to my summer birthday party; my birthday's in December. I figured if I made the party sound inviting, they wouldn't oppose my crossing their property in search of my kitty.

While the plan appeared to work and I retrieved my kitty without incident, I experienced a slight squirming inside like the wiggle of a little worm.

By the age of five, this little girl had learned she couldn't approach people in an honest and direct way, that people couldn't be trusted with her needs. Why did she feel she had to manipulate people to get what she wanted?

Recovering from alcoholism at age 44, I discovered what had compromised my ability to trust and to sustain the in-to-me-see necessary to connect with others and to myself.

Anxiety, depression, and a cancer diagnosis would also begin to make sense.

The *Story* of Me: Early Signs of Obsession and Compulsion

I was born Helen Loraine Foster on December 22, 1944, in a coal mining town named Minto in southern New Brunswick, Canada. My parents were nearly 42 years old at my birth and had had two daughters before me: one stillborn and one named Diane who lived only two days. I would not know of Diane until after my parents' deaths in a car accident when I was 40 years old.

As an only child to middle-aged parents, I learned how to be alone and to feel deeply without interruption. Nature and pets gave me a sense of family and belonging. My earliest memories were of pet cats, a dog named Timmy, and a French Roman Catholic best friend, two years younger than English Protestant me.

No Fights, Loraine

I recall my mother telling me each time I went out to play, "No fights, Loraine." As an only child with no big brothers, I sometimes felt the need to fight for my place in Saturday matinee line-ups or for my turn to slide on the hills.

One time, I recall running home to get one of my father's guns … he was a hunter … in order to put an end to a fight with a boy who rammed into my lower back on purpose while sliding too closely behind me.

My mother stood in the way of this plan. I often wonder today if she had not been at home, if a gun had been available and loaded, would I have been a 12-year-old on the news? It's possible; I was really mad.

Discrimination

I remember being sent home by two Roman Catholic women who told me I couldn't slide on *their* hill, a municipally-cleared road, because I wasn't Catholic. My best friend refused to continue sliding if I couldn't.

When I told my mother, she was furious. She went to the hill to wait for these nurses to return from work and told them *what's what.* Then I was even more scared to go sliding in case I encountered one of the nurses who now knew I had told my mother.

I remember this same best friend being afraid to lift our Bible while helping me dust because of her understanding of her priest's teachings. She also had to make *the sign of the cross* when she walked in front of her church.

Obsessive Thinking and Compulsive Behaviours

A particularly painful memory occurred when I had to return a tadpole to the watery basement remains of a store across the street that had burned down by what mum called *Jewish Lightning.* When I threw the tadpole back, I thought I hadn't done it right and I felt obsessive guilt and torment over it.

I had a hard time with colouring books too. If I coloured outside the line even once, I had to turn the page and try to forget about it. One time, the whole colouring book had to go to the side porch leading outdoors and it still bothered me. I felt as if I could foam at the mouth like a dog with rabies; it was that intense at times.

Another obsessive compulsive moment overtook me around age eight while I was crossing town one afternoon. I felt compelled to circle a telephone pole alongside the sidewalk three times. While I didn't want the embarrassment of being seen, I knew if I didn't do it, something beyond my control, something I wouldn't like, would happen.

First Regret

The only bad deed I felt shame in doing was trying to convince a poor boy next door I had made chocolate milk for him during my *baking* with mud and water days.

First Mood-altering Experience

I remember getting dressed up and being at a parade for the 1953 Coronation of a queen named Elizabeth. Magical ... the thought of a real live queen ... much scrapbooking pleasure followed and I recalled the scent of a glue that made me feel good.

Fear of Others Than Us

When I found my father's black armband in a drawer, blackouts were explained and I was told the only *bad guys* were red and called *Russians* and they lived far, far away ... so not to worry.

At the Saturday afternoon cowboy and Indian matinees, I grew terrified the cowboys would be ambushed and wanted them to hide behind big rocks I saw on the screen. I soon caught on to who the good cowboy was; he rode a white horse and wore a white hat. The bad cowboy rode a black horse and wore a black hat.

Safety of the 1950s

My father would give me the store's deposit in a cloth bag and I would walk across town to the bank with it when I was just a little girl. I also worked in the store, pulling the right-hand side lever on the cash register to make the drawer pop out, and I pumped gas for American tourists with the odd green money. They talked about our coloured leaves.

Que Sera, Sera was a song playing on the radio a lot; another was *Love and Marriage*. We kids sang these, knowing the words, not the meaning.

A Sister for Me?

Mum gave me a *shiny* and two brown pennies to buy milk for recess in grade two. I'd buy one chocolate for me and one white for another little girl. She had *lost* her parents and was being raised by her sister, a nurse, another sister and a brother.

One Sunday afternoon, Mum, Dad, and I drove to this girl's home and a long talk ensued. I desperately wanted a sister and this girl was allowed, for a time, to live at our house. I remember we received identical Christmas gifts: a chenille aquamarine housecoat with pink flowers, watches, stocking stuffers and all.

Then one day got serious for me. The girl's two grown-up sisters came to our house to talk with Mum and Dad about moving away to Alberta. The girl and I went for a long walk and I tried desperately, tiringly, to convince her to stay with us.

She chose to move away with her family. I felt devastated. I had lost the chance to have a sister.

Roots of a Nomadic Life

When I was about to enter grade four at age nine, we moved from Minto to Fredericton, thirty miles away from where Dad owned what I later learned was the first Canadian Tire Store in the Maritimes.

This meant a daily commute for my father and new people in my little life. There was no best friend and no Timmy. Mum insisted he stay behind with the store as his home.

"I hate Fredericton." I posted signs on pillows and wrote this on the chalkboard I used to teach imaginary students in the sun porch in Minto. I travelled back to Minto with my Dad on Saturdays, back to my best friend and my dog. I lived for Saturdays.

Lo and behold, we moved back to Minto for grades seven and eight. Now, there was a girl who was seemingly smarter than I and might take first place. I remember a spelling test in grade seven when I obsessed about the word judgement ... whether it had an *E* after the *G* and the fact a mistake would mean my first score less than 100 on a spelling test. The mental agony lasted forever. To this day, I pause and have a problem with that word. I have blocked from memory whether I scored 100 or not.

In grade eight, a weird teacher called a *Pentecost* came to class one day with a brightly-coloured garter snake wrapped around the fingers of one hand. She insisted we handle it before passing it on to the student behind us. Although the feeling of being forced unnerved me, I would never have said no to a teacher.

I remember my first school dance. I wore black patent shoes, a pale blue fleck suit, and a white blouse. A boy walked me home, and my parents started talking about getting me back to Fredericton, to more suitable companions than Minto could offer. What?

I had always been first or second of my class in Minto. I won the IODE prize for coming first in grade two, and two women delivered books to the darkened living room where I was confined with the measles. *Winnie the Pooh* and *The Secret Garden* became meaningful in midlife along with the *Tao of Pooh*.

Back in Fredericton and in grade nine, I got taken out of class one day without explanation and put into a room with other students to write a standardized test with strict time limits. I felt severely unnerved by this whole ordeal, particularly when I didn't get to finish it … a first for me. I went home crying to my mother, saying I couldn't return to school because everybody would think I didn't belong. I remember mother explaining to me that either Churchill or Einstein didn't do well on these tests. Because my mother had been a rural school teacher before marrying my father, I trusted her and returned to school.

I still travelled to Minto with my father on Saturdays to be with my best friend and my dog. One Saturday, Timmy and I found that my best friend had a best friend too and that hurt … a lot!

So, I tried to be friends with my best friend's new best friend but things were never the same.

Name Change and Self Conscious Teen Years

At the completion of grade nine and about to enter high school, my friends began to call me *Lori* instead of *Loraine*. I didn't think to object.

In grade ten, a friend who wanted to be on the cheerleading team asked me to try out with her. I got chosen; she didn't. So, there I was by default, liking the feeling of having been chosen, feeling bad for my friend, and feeling uncomfortable about appearing publicly as part of the team.

I was overly self-conscious. When I saw a popular boy looking at the surface of our indoor skating rink, I would lose the ability to skate and grab hold of the sideboards while trying to look like I was taking a break.

Need to Belong

It was also in grade ten that our homeroom teacher left a pile of files on her desk and we learned our IQ scores from the standardized testing in grade nine. I fit right in with my friends at a point or two above average. That felt really comforting.

Although school was easy for me, I aimed for lower grades to help me fit in. I didn't want to be at the top of the class, only high enough to qualify for university. That worked and my popularity increased.

Dieting and What's Real?

I began dieting at age 15, eating only two boiled eggs for breakfast or Jell-O without the whipped topping when at restaurants with friends. I recall looking into a shop mirror while trying on size eight pants and knowing both my mother and the saleslady were lying to me when they said I didn't look big.

Grades 11 and 12 were a blur of obsessing over my looks and a certain boy. My cousin and I walked past his house some nights. The endless *talking about* blurred the lines between reality and fantasy.

Summer Job and Need to Get Creative

At age sixteen, I began summertime work as playground supervisor for the City Recreation Department while also training for a Bronze Medallion so I could lifeguard at the city pool. Successful, I began lifeguard work the summer of grade 11.

When the Department was asked to provide a lifeguard for the Girl Guide Summer Camp, I was chosen without consultation or job description.

I didn't know I'd be responsible for teaching the girls a variety of swimming strokes, achievable at varying distances, as well as how to dive.

This was to prepare the guides to attain badges upon successful examination by a University of New Brunswick physical education professor.

The problem was, there was no equipment for measuring lengths and no platform for diving.

The lodge, where we ate, had acquired a new fridge, so I made floaters from pieces of solid foam and found rope to tie to a lakeshore tree that sloped outward into the water.

Then I swam with rope and floaters and sank a boulder at a familiar pool length distance. This was used for both short and longer distance badges dependent on the number of lengths swam.

For diving lessons, I found a leaky wooden rowboat. The quarter pie-shaped bow served as a platform from which one guide could learn how to dive while a second guide bailed out the incoming water with a tin can.

It worked. The guides were examined on their swimming and diving skills and I looked forward to entering university.

In September, as a physical education (Phys Ed) student and I walked across campus, he told me one of his professors had taught a class on what can be done when there's no equipment to work with. The professor referred to the experience he had had at a Girl Guide camp that summer.

I'm not a Competitor.

This same Phys Ed student told me that more girls were needed for the varsity swim team and that I should try out even though tryouts had already taken place. I ventured over to the indoor pool in the basement of a men's residence, jumped in, swam, and left.

The following Saturday, at a rugby game, one of the girls from the pool came over to me and said the swim coach wanted to meet the new girl who had been at the pool.

I met with the coach. He paced along as I swam a length or two and asked what size bathing suit to order.

When the women's team captain challenged me to a *swim off* alone at the pool and I beat her, it didn't feel good or right to me. I learned that I liked swimming, not competing.

Not knowing how to get out of things, I did swim competition for a bit.

Magnetic Pull: Series of Coincidences that Led to a Husband

One fall day in 1962, while walking toward campus, I felt a strong magnetic pull in the direction of a white car stopped at a residential intersection. It appeared to be a businessman wearing a beige trench in the driver's seat. I continued walking.

Still on the swim team, I was up on the starting block waiting for the starter gun when I felt drawn to look to where a male I didn't know stood among the small crowd of spectators. I swam fast and got out of the pool, curious to find out what had drawn my attention like that. He was gone.

I sat with my cousin and a few university cheerleaders gathered at the Student Centre cafeteria. They were talking about a hockey player they found attractive. Much to their astonishment, I had no idea who he was.

My date for Winter Carnival was a swimmer on the men's varsity team. Last minute, the coach chose him for competition at McGill University. I told a first year classmate from northern New Brunswick that I now had no date. He told a fourth year student from a small town near his and this person wanted to meet me.

As I emerged from the ladies' bathroom, I was introduced to the person I had observed in the white car, had looked for at the swim meet, and had heard about in the cafeteria.

Although we dated while seeing others, when I ran into him while out on a date, he told me to get rid of the guy. I did, by shamefully lying to my date so I could get home early and meet up with him.

At the end of the university year, when I assumed he had left town, I unexpectedly ran into him on Queen Street and had a chance to say good-bye.

While waiting for exam results to be posted on campus, Mum told me I had missed a long distance call from a male.

Long distance calls were costly and rare in the 60s; in fact, at age 18, I had never received one.

Assuming I knew who the call was from, I wrote a letter and put it in the red mailbox on the corner. A second long distance call revealed the original caller had been a first year student enquiring if exam results had been posted

Feelings of Obsession and Powerlessness

Feeling embarrassed and ashamed for having exposed my feelings in a letter, I waited for the postman and tried to persuade him to return my letter. He couldn't and wouldn't.

I felt immobilized while watching and waiting for mail delivery. A letter did come, followed by a summer visit. That fall he left university because his grades weren't good enough to allow him to play varsity hockey.

We continued to be in contact through calls and letters and I visited at Christmas.

I could no longer focus on my studies and told my best friend that I preferred to be run over by a truck than not be with this person.

I felt powerless over my own life, unable and unwilling to fight it.

I left university in my second year, converted to Catholicism, and married the person I was obsessed with.

I believed this was love, that it was *meant to be*. The song of my early years, *Love and Marriage*, was playing out in real time at age 19.

Disowned

Although my first and best childhood friend, like a sister to me, had been a French Roman Catholic, I was disowned for falling in love with a French Roman Catholic.

My father, who had spoken maybe a hundred words to me before this, calmly told me, "I'd rather see you dead and in your grave."

He considered this a betrayal.

My parents did not attend the wedding.

Coincidences and Cancer Diagnosis

I assumed a difficult marriage of 11 years, teaching high school, and helping on the family farm accounted for my feeling physically tired and emotionally weary.

My teenaged babysitter insisted I see her doctor who had moved from a large American city to a town south of ours.

"You have sarcoma in situ and a choice to make: conical cervical removal if you want a third child or a hysterectomy. If you choose the first, you have to be able to accept the risk of postponing the hysterectomy."

At 30 years old, I had two sons, age ten and six.

What this doctor didn't tell me was that a series of pap smears performed on an earlier patient showed him how quickly these cells could change. Instead, he adeptly guided my choosing an immediate hysterectomy without scaring me to death before he could perform it.

While practicing in New York, he had worked with Can Cope, unheard of in New Brunswick in 1975. The first person at my bedside following the operation was the woman he had previously treated.

This earlier patient had survived and he knew a living testimony would benefit me more than any assurances he could offer.

The doctor also knew I'd need this as he had found an unexpected growth during surgery.

While my husband had been told of the growth, I was not, only that I had to remain in hospital a harrowing 10 days while awaiting lab results and any indications for further treatment.

Following the operation, my husband visited me at the hospital stating, "I'm going to Florida this winter. If you don't want to come, I'll find someone who will."

I felt a slight jolt but also felt appeased that his plan sort of considered me. Our relationship's survival appeared to exist on a precarious and volatile energy.

Lab results were okay. I got to go home rather than to a hospital in the southern part of the province for further treatment.

We went to Florida.

A Marriage in Trouble: Fusion (Codependency) and Rage-aholism

Age 30 and 11 years married, I naively hoped the cancer would provide a wake-up call that would miraculously improve the marriage, make my husband more loving, less rageful and scary.

I didn't know how to hold onto myself and be in a marriage where I felt scared.

Three years before the cancer, at age 27, I had discovered alcohol could calm my fear when, from the kitchen window, I would spot my husband's angry body language as he walked from the barn to the house.

Neither cancer nor alcohol could fix the marriage. Hope for change only lasted a few weeks. The marriage was tumultuous, even physical.

My best friends and support system were two fellow teachers. Without their support, I wouldn't be here today.

I recall a poignant moment when one of them asked, "Do you think this is love or dependency?"

I had no idea I suffered from codependency, an outer fixation so strong I was losing the vital connection to my inner sounding board, to my own anger that would tell me to get out.

I had become dependent upon, obsessed with, and reactive to the person I had married at 19.

Many years later, I learned abuse could only happen where there is a perception of inequality. That perception was mine. I saw myself as Pepsi to his Coke. I had made him my God.

He once told me, "Not everything I say is God's word." To one of my friends, he remarked, "Lori doesn't defend herself … I wish she would."

I saw family safety as dependent on my not provoking his unpredictable rage.

While developing protective antennae for cues to his anger, I was going numb inside.

What had become of the little girl who was born connected, animated, feeling *All is well?*

I had become a person without a Self who would be looking for herself six years later in self-help books.

Serendipity Ended the Marriage; it Remains the Most Painful Loss.

At 18 years of marriage, a phone bill I wouldn't have normally looked at revealed my husband was having an affair. I saw in him the familiar signs of obsession I had felt.

While I hoped he'd feel guilty enough not to act out violently against my leaving with our sons, I still took precautions as the three of us left town for my parents' home 150 miles south.

The marriage ended at Christmas in 1982, seven years after the cancer diagnosis and ten years into my progressive trouble with alcohol.

My sons, 17 and 13, would live six long years without a functioning mother before I could admit defeat and seek treatment.

Their father and the woman he had had an affair with were living in their childhood home … a house that no longer felt like a home to them.

That is the greatest tragedy of all and the hardest personal truth that cannot be undone.

Compulsion to Act that Couldn't be Ignored

On August 28, 1984, my mother's birthday, I arrived home from a teaching job at the community college, had a couple of drinks, and proceeded to drive across the river before nine. My parents went to bed early.

Soon after leaving my driveway, I felt a strong insistence that I turn around and retrieve an unmailed letter I had written to my father in September 1981.

Since the letter was written before the marriage break up and the move to my parents' hometown, I wasn't sure I could find it.

My lips moved in argument with this insistence, strongly felt, despite my having consumed three double vodkas. I finally agreed to go back and look in two places.

I found the letter, put it in a sealed envelope, and told my mother to give it to my father after I left; I was afraid of being judged too emotional.

The letter thanked my father for letting eight-year-old me and my best friend sleep overnight in a cardboard box our new fridge had come in. I also confessed to why he never killed a deer when he took me hunting; I had eaten crunchy apples and stepped on dry twigs to warn the deer. I told him, "Never fear that you failed as a father because you didn't."

I called my mother each day after teaching and sure enough, my father's initial reaction was, "Loraine must have been very emotional when she wrote this."

I stayed away for a couple of days before returning to an extended as-far-as-the-arm-could-reach handshake from my father while he thanked me for a lovely letter.

Deaths of Both Parents

Popping over for lunch with my parents, I found Mum dressed for a doctor's appointment. When I offered to take her, she declined, saying she felt well enough to sit in a waiting room for hours and Dad could drive her.

Home from work that afternoon, I called my mother. There was no answer. After trying a number of times, I called the next-door neighbour who insisted I come over to her place. Telling her I had no time for a visit, I asked if Dad's car was in the driveway. If Mum had to go into the hospital, Dad would be flustered. They were 81 and 82 years old.

Unable to get past this neighbour's insistence, I went to her place, thinking I'd check on my parents myself. At her home, while beginning to realize something might have happened to both Mum AND Dad, I saw a patrol car roll up in front of her house. A white-collared minister sat in the passenger seat.

The first thing I felt compelled to do was call a friend and let her know I couldn't attend the Kenny Rogers concert, that she had to give my ticket to someone else because my parents weren't feeling well.

I don't remember anything said to me after that. I know I refused to identify the bodies and that my lower jaw kept moving without ceasing for hours. It only stopped when I held it with my left hand.

I was in shock, no doubt, and wouldn't you know, the craziest cousin arrived first and tried to get me to go look at caskets. Thank God I had Vodka!!! She even moved in to sleep with me for a few days and I awoke one night to hear her fake crying. I pretended to be sleeping and quickly got out from under her *care*.

Following the double funeral, a neighbour told me that Dad, a man of few words, had told her of a lovely letter he had received from his daughter.

That letter, given to him through Mum two weeks before they died, saved my life because I don't believe I could have gotten sober without having told him what I needed to.

I had shut down my feelings in my teens because expressing them had caused my father to ask himself how he had failed as a father.

September 24, 1984, I asked a friend for a lift to my parents' house, so I could pick up my car.

There it sat, in the driveway.

As I got into the car, I noticed a newspaper on the passenger seat. Its date, September 14, 1984 … the date my parents died.

PART II

HEALING

Sobriety

From my first drink at age 27, eight years into married life, until age 43, I tried to recover the feelings of safety and *yummy in the tummy* of that little girl at the lake.

It took more and more alcohol to chase after that lost connection until I could no longer believe the lie that alcohol could get me there.

There had to be another way.

I sobered up in 1988 through a combination of counselling, a 28-day treatment program, and Twelve-step meetings.

The Drug and Alcohol outpatient counsellor, a recovering alcoholic herself, said, "Thank God you had alcohol."

My head pivoted on my shoulders like Linda Blair's in the movie *The Exorcist* as I looked around for anyone who might have overheard what she had said. I was afraid she'd be fired.

Her comment hadn't come about from any deep disclosures of mine although she was aware of my having lost both parents.

It would be a decade or more before her haunting statement began to make sense.

The Outpatient Counsellor got me admitted to a Residential Treatment Centre. While there, a therapist asked if I would tell the group what I had told her. "If my parents were still alive, I would not have embarrassed them by entering treatment for alcoholism." I refused. I had just realized this myself.

Since then, I have tried to come to some kind of understanding as to how this only child to non-drinking Baptist parents could bring such shame upon herself and her parents if they were alive.

Recovery took me on a dark journey. The first flashback came while I was at the treatment facility. I was no longer trying to be strong through booze. On a subconscious level, I must have felt safe to receive hidden memories.

The plug had been in the jug for maybe three weeks now, and the sewer was beginning to back up and overflow, ready or not. I certainly didn't trust ANYONE enough to talk about this.

As to the *why* of alcoholism, we're told not to ask about that in early recovery. It's possible I was born to a mother who could not mirror her inner connection. My own has been very fragile.

In class, when a therapist asked each of us how we thought we ended up in treatment, most male answers were DUI, threat of jail, or threat of job loss. Mine was, "The pilot light is nearly out in the cold, damp furnace inside me."

Much later, I came to realize this was a recognition of my inner link to a Higher Power. As an early childhood sexual abuse survivor, my ability to relate to anything associated with *Higher*, or *Power*, or *God* as male had been compromised.

Both my personal and professional experiences have since confirmed the survivor's psyche will only reveal its truth when the person feels adequate safety and support.

Out of Victimhood through a Twelve-step Program

<u>Please Note</u>: No individual has the capacity to represent any Twelve-step Program. I write from personal, ever-evolving interpretation.

Up to age 44, I had unknowingly viewed life from a victim mindset.

The Twelve-step Program took me from victim thinking to recognizing I played a participatory role in my life. Part of the process required an honest and thorough look at my life, patterns and motivating factors. Following that, and in consultation with a sponsor, I was to make amends to those I had harmed.

Not a great follower of suggestions, I made a first amend MY way without consulting a sponsor.

Unaware of codependency issues, I wrote my former husband to apologize for having caused my own maltreatment during the marriage as well as for his having had an affair. In the letter, I expressed gratitude to the woman he had the affair with as it had contributed to my being where I was now in my life. He accepted this apology and said it made this woman feel better too. I told him I did it for my own recovery. I don't think either of us understood this at the time, but it was a start and I am still sober.

Beginning to see how deficient I was in regards to emotional bonding, I wrote to my older son to assure him of his lovability.

I believe the amends to my younger son came more in the form of demonstrating change on a daily basis, passing on what I was learning.

The Search for a God of my understanding

As *my* understanding of AA's first step expanded beyond my powerlessness over alcohol, I began to see myself as a recovering food-aholic, men-aholic, intellect-aholic, periodic work-aholic, read-aholic, recent Netflix-aholic … still living the all or nothing, out of balance, obsessive compulsive life.

As far back as the 70s, I recall joking, "I talk too much, eat too much, smoke too much and drink too much," while an ominous bell peeled through my nervous humour.

I've since come to realize that I, of myself, couldn't have done anything about it. "Lori, you can't change yourself," a metaphysical reverend friend still reminds me today.

My current interpretation of AA's first three Steps are:

1. i can't.

2. IT can. (i.e. Another Source of Power)

3. Think i'll let IT. (as i understand IT at any given time).

Step 3, found on page 59 of *Alcoholics Anonymous* 3rd ed. states: "Made a decision to turn our will and our lives over to the care of God *as we understood Him*."

I had difficulty with religious referencing to a male god, so *as we understood* helped.

In frustration, I sometimes angrily and irreverently joked that the God of my understanding seemed to be on a long Coffee Break!

Following Residential Alcohol Treatment, I attended Twelve-step meetings several times a week for a number of years all the while looking for connection with this *Power of my understanding.*

I Knew What I Didn't Want

My not wanting a relationship with the God of Religion ran deeper than a gender issue.

What I heard at Sunday church service did nothing to endear me to the stalker-type that sees everything, that you can't hide from even under the bed or in the closet. This *God* I heard of as a five-year-old terrified me.

That fear snowballed into feelings of guilt. *I must have done something wrong* turned into *something is wrong with me*, then into *I deserve judgement, so I may as well get ahead of this by judging myself. Remember, you picked up a safety pin on a sidewalk and it didn't belong to you?*

Worse still, I learned He allowed His own son to be killed for those very sins of ours. He wouldn't even respond to his son's prayer for help. No point in asking. No expectation of compassion either. The Power dynamic was pretty obvious to me and it didn't look so good.

Powers of My Own and my Parents' Making

While rummaging in the hall closet under a hand-made wooden two-step, I found a big unopened box of chocolate-covered stale vanilla creams. I remember eating several while *yummy in the tummy* feelings spread through me.

This was my first privately held, secret stash I could count on, return to, and know it was there for me. Little did I realize the marvellous sugar-fat combo would become a god for me.

My mother bought these chocolates on sale, hence dried up. Did she, too, want to feel some security, some control, by saving, even hoarding money? Was this her defense against fully trusting this scary god we learned of in church? Mum taught Sunday School.

Dad ate ice cream alone during the night. Only he knew how much or how often, as he quickly replaced the huge empty tubs with new ones. He often denied himself a treat when we stopped at the new soft ice cream place while he bought cones for Mum and me, even seconds if I wanted.

While his doctor issued caution regarding his triglyceride levels, Dad was an anxious sort, and I guess he took comfort in his sugar-fat combo despite health warnings. Eating during the night seemed to help him sleep, too, by numbing his anxiety a bit.

He once declared that if he were a drinking man, he most likely would have been an alcoholic.

We never talked about any of this while they were alive, but I had to take a look back when face-to-face with my own full-blown alcoholism at age 44.

Insecurity Led to the Power of Control.

Grade 10, age fifteen, my first *no-kiss boyfriend* gravitated toward another girl. There was no breakup, but I knew I wasn't worthy of him. Even though I was an average-size girl, I assumed there was something wrong with me. *Maybe I needed to lose weight. After all, look at supermodel Twiggy.*

My ego masqueraded as a *God in Control,* appearing capable of power over my empty and hungry feelings, over when to deprive and when to give to myself.

Having lost connection with my true Nature, this misguided dependency on a dissociated self as God, caused a lot of suffering.

So what now? Reconnection Begins and More is Revealed.

Because strangers in Twelve-step meetings were willing to share from their core, I became able to find mine.

Finally, the mirroring I had been missing.

The pilot light, first noticed at the Treatment Centre, began to burn brighter.

I belonged.

Sobriety gave me the opportunity to access further healing.

In 1989, I read *Love, Medicine and Miracles* by Dr. Bernie Siegel.

A seeming link between cancer, female anatomy related to reproduction, and a chronically non-nurturing relationship got my attention.

I attended the author's weekend conference on cancer and healing in

Toronto. This is my partially paraphrased understanding.

Dr. Siegel asked the attendees at the Friday night pre-conference a question. "If you got a diagnosis giving you six months to live, that's about one hundred and eighty days, how many of you would say *yes* to a day of helping a friend move?"

He explained that if we say *yes* and need to say *no*, we are giving ourselves the message that we don't matter, that we don't have value.

Those who were able to be true to their inner selves while responding to the request were told they didn't need to stay for the full weekend as they were not at risk for cancer.

While the mind will tell us changing stories, like one version at 3:15 PM and another at 3:17 PM, Dr. Siegel proposed the body doesn't lie. If it feels dis-ease and is not listened to, it will eventually act out this dis-ease by manifesting disease.

I stayed the full weekend.

At first, I thought the cancer-causing, non-nurturing relationship had been between my husband and me. It wasn't. It was the discordant relationship between my mind and body. My dissociated self was out of alignment with my true Nature which was trying to send signals to my mind through my body.

Dr. Siegel taught us a way to realign.

He suggested we check in with ourselves five to six times a day to see if what we're doing is in harmony with our true Nature.

If disharmony is felt, we have three choices: Stop it, Resolve it, or Change it.

I put this learning into practice. I started making a three-hour stew for my two sons and myself. When the sun came out, I began to feel conflicted, a bit resentful, victimized because I now wanted to be outdoors.

When I noticed self-pity, I put the stew on hold in the fridge, to be continued later … or not.

I credit this learning with giving me a way out of years of resentment and self-pity, two terms tightly linked in the victim mindset.

More significantly, page 64 of *Alcoholics Anonymous*, 3rd ed. states,

"Resentment is the 'number one' offender. It destroys more alcoholics than anything else." I had to get this or die.

Victim thinking and attitudes underlie alcoholic drinking: *Poor me, poor me, pour me a drink.*

While I don't like labels, such as *victim*, naming it allowed me to see it.

Unintentional Parental Inadequacies and Long Term Effects

Insufficient Socialization and Bonding

I had always felt adrift, lonely, insecure … like a barnacle looking for a rock to attach to.

Because my mother wasn't comfortable with social gatherings, I wasn't adequately socialized. I felt like a skittish barn kitty around people.

While I had existed physically within the sphere of my parents, my cake remained gooey in the middle. No real bond was formed. I didn't learn if, how, or where I fit.

Parents who weren't Parented

My mother, the last of nine children, said her mother had run out of steam by the time she came along. She said she grew up much like a weed.

A Parent's Unresolved Fears get Passed on

My mother's unresolved fear of dentists had an unintended effect on me. I wasn't taught personal hygiene or grooming. The lack of consistent dental care and dental check-ups resulted in tooth extractions in my teens. Ashamed, I began to smile differently to hide this.

Where My Expression of Feelings Ends and Fusion (Co-dependency) Begins

My father considered emotional expression to be unladylike, a sign of instability.

As a teen, when I poked a mascara brush into my eye and said a four-letter word meaning excrement, my father went to his room for two days.

I later found a two-page type-written letter on the dresser in my bedroom. In it, he was asking himself how he had failed as a father, that I would express myself in this way or shriek in delight while listening to the top record in the countdown of the top ten as it played on the radio.

From this, I learned I was responsible for other people's feelings and that I was a disappointment. It's called fusion, co-dependency, a symbiotic relationship. Not a great relationship template.

Neglect

While I may have appeared aloof, self-centred, at times inconsiderate, possibly even spoiled, personal discovery work, plus years of professional work with others point to an emotionally neglected child.

Although an intelligent and educated adult, I didn't realize others cared, that others wanted to be called when I would be late. At age 46, I experienced a Kodak Moment when my daughter-in-law asked to be informed once I knew the date I'd be moving across the country, so she and my older son "could prepare their hearts". Say what?

When a person speaks of a spoiled child, are they really describing symptoms of neglect? Did the parent compensate with gifts and money because they were never shown how to parent, or did they, like my mother, *just grow like a weed* because their mother had *run out of steam*?

Because the neglect wasn't physical, I didn't identify it as such until I was in late adulthood. My inadequacy in relationships found me temporarily homeless at the age of 57.

In 2002, I attended a conference in Vancouver focused on body-centred therapy in healing trauma and Post Traumatic Stress Disorder (PTSD).

Dr. Bessel van der Kolk, an expert in this area, put on a PowerPoint presentation to illustrate the effects of various types of childhood abuse. Neglect can show up as a life unravelling in late adulthood.

Both Dr. van der Kolk and Dr. John Briere, who also presented at this conference, are worth researching.

Awareness of a Compromised Ability to Bond

Through attending Twelve-step meetings for a problem with alcohol, I became aware that alcohol was but a symptom.

I began to feel connected and accepted by strangers gathered together for the purpose of healing. When I spoke of an earlier inability to adequately bond with my first born, I was told, "You were damaged." I had little understanding of what *damaged* meant. In the same way a person doesn't know they're depressed until the depression lifts, I didn't know I had never experienced love. Without a contrast, I was unable to see it.

At age 47, I told a friend I had seen a look of love and acceptance in the eyes of a recovering heroin addict I didn't even know. Gasping, she exclaimed, "You mean you never saw that look in your father's eyes?"

It wasn't until age 53 and the failure of a final attempt at relationship, that I came to terms with the limitations of my original relationship template. Decades of growth and learning had not overcome this deficit.

Finding this difficult to accept, I consulted a psychic who put it simply, "Dearie, your chooser is broken."

While I may not like or agree with reality, I do have to accept it in order to do things differently.

Autobiography in Five Short Chapters, a poem by Portia Nelson, best describes the process of change.

The Gradual, Almost Gentle, Process of Uncovering Early Sexual Abuse

It sometimes felt as though I were opening up a luxurious seasonal home where the sofas and stuffed chairs were under white dust sheets, and I was removing only one dust cover at a time.

The uncovering, while unsettling, began in mid-life when my psyche was strong enough and I had adequate emotional support.

My first memory of pre-verbal sexual abuse came in a flashback while at a residential treatment program for alcohol dependency.

I was 44 years old and in a non-smoking building. It so jarred me that I risked smoking a cigarette in the bathroom immediately following the flashback that awoke me in the middle of the night.

I told no one but did break up with a boyfriend I was seeing at the time, telling him, "This is not about alcohol and I don't know where this is going, but I can't be in a relationship right now."

The next dust cover came off when I, not a *squeezer*, reached out with my left hand while carrying items in my right and squeezed a sponge in the aisle display at a local box store.

I immediately flushed red, felt hot, dropped the items I was carrying, left the store, drove home, and rushed up the stairs, straight down the hall to my bedroom.

I knew something was wrong, but I didn't understand what.

I was in my first year of alcohol recovery with no trauma language. I didn't realize I had been triggered and that another memory was rising to the surface. Although I was attending weekly post treatment counselling for alcohol dependency, I didn't see any reason to bring this forward in a counselling session.

In addition to attending Twelve-step meetings, I participated in private weekly meetings with four other women focused on healing and recovery.

One of the women was thinking of taking Art Therapy, so I accompanied her to Mount Allison University where the University of Toronto was putting on a recruitment-type weekend seminar.

When they presented drawings done by young sexual abuse survivors, I saw how trauma had caused consciousness to leave one child's body. She painted herself seated up on the limb of a tree outside her blackened bedroom window.

Weeks later, a different member of the group disclosed childhood sexual abuse, so I gave her a flyer on an upcoming weekend intensive I planned to attend as a healer, part of my Masters of Education in Guidance and Counselling (M.Ed.).

That night, I awoke in physical pain that remained long enough for me to realize it was a childhood body memory.

In the morning, I called the university counsellor to amend my attendee application from healer to victim, feeling driven to correct this immediately.

The counsellor recognized the significance of this disclosure. I didn't. When she offered me an appointment to come in and talk about this, I told her that wasn't necessary.

An M.Ed. classmate presented a study of female alcoholics. A piece of research was circulated among us stating 80% of these women had been sexually abused. I remember thinking, "Thank God. I don't have that to deal with."

During the weekend intensive on sexual abuse, I arrived early for a social evening and nervously wandered over to a table displaying the university counsellor's recently completed thesis on childhood sexual abuse. It was open to two pages listing thirteen symptoms. I had eleven of the thirteen. I wanted to run. Others began arriving.

While I spoke to no one about this, I did begin to journal. Years later, as a counsellor, I would recommend *The Courage to Heal* by Ellen Bass & Laura Davis.

As M.Ed. students, we were taught to watch for symptoms of possible sexual abuse in teens: sexually provocative behaviours, really tight or really loose clothing. Long sleeves in warm temperatures could be hiding cutting activity, an attempt to self-regulate inner pain.

Eating Disorders can be symptomatic of sexual abuse.

What My Eating Disorder is Revealing

While too young to have awareness of earlier trauma underlying my anxiously obsessive nature, I found myself in church sitting next to a woman with red plastic earrings. I felt so obsessed, I had to sit on my hands so I wouldn't reach up and touch them.

For 57 years, I've tried to manage my feelings and my weight. I've tried smoking, physician-prescribed amphetamines, a dozen popular diets, and joining a certain weight loss program 19 times.

This struggle, even greater than the one with alcohol that lasted 17 years, had broken me repeatedly and enough that I had to become open to another way of being in life.

While alcohol can be eliminated, food cannot.

The eating disorder forced me to loosen my barnacling (codependency) to outer forms for my comfort, safety, and guidance, and to increasingly rely on an inner connection … to return to the natural ability I had as a young child … to live from the inside out.

Since I am a work in progress, the following is intended to be *descriptive* rather than *prescriptive.*

1. Who cares to admit complete defeat?

Until I was done *trying* my many ways to achieve control over my use of alcohol, I was unwilling to be open to a different way. The same holds true for the many repetitions of *trying* to manage weight.

2. Am I done *trying* to have personal power/control/attempts at manageability on this issue?

I have to be radically honest with my innermost being that *I can't do this*.

3. Am I *willing* to question a perception of myself as a personal and separate source, capable of self-management through willpower?

A temporarily held illusion of control through willpower kept me repeating similar attempts: *This time, it will be different … I can achieve the goal I want.*

Thinking I want something, someone, a certain situational outcome *other than what is* can set me on this course again. Paradoxically, repetitious failure *can* waken me from the grip of my rogue ego mind.

4. Am I *willing* to be open to a different way?

Only after I've tried 17 of my ego's ways first, thank you very much. That these ways have not had any lasting effect would be allowing Truth to get in the way of my rationalizations.

5. Will I *allow* for the possibility that my Nature, my intuitive Self may be Streaming Universal Power *through* and *as* me?

If I'm honest with myself, I do get hints and nudges from within that seem to run counter-intuitive to my ego thoughts … such as *Should I have cheese on my burger?* might come up as *Yes* when my Super ego would say, *You shouldn't even be having that burger.*

An intuitive resonance I experienced upon hearing the name British Columbia (BC) in 1952, became a trip across Canada in 1990 with the feeling I was coming home.

An intuitive picture of hanging up a counselling shingle occurred during an M.Ed. class in 1989. I went into private practice in 2002.

Some flashes materialize almost immediately if they're about something simple. When the flash involves other people, it may take two years or more to show up.

6. Then I may be open to a pathway to my Nature and my natural weight.

If I'm willing to trust inner promptings despite temporary fear or even the appearance of weight gain, then I'm open to a different way. Old concepts such as a specific size of clothing or a specific number on the scale have to go.

7. Ask … Listen … Follow

I choose to check within without using what I think I know because that judgment comes from all the previous mental conditioning, which never did work in the end.

8. I expect to feel rattled as previously-conditioned concepts float to the surface for release. (Hot air balloon comes to mind)

Ego rises and I sometimes feel scared while needing to trust inner promptings that go against old concepts about certain foods. This is where I learn to discern between conditioned thinking and inner guidance. Frequently this requires rigorous honesty with my deepest Self.

9. I TRUST that what appears to be counter-intuitive may actually be counter-conditioning.

I came to realize I wasn't hungry at noon but rather at 2:30, that I might want almonds or oatmeal at dinnertime.

10. I clear my mind of expectations *if* I choose to get on a scale.

If I feel conditioned guilt over what I've eaten and get on the scale expecting a number that reflects this … that's precisely what I'll see. Beliefs project outward and reflect back.

If I clear all concepts and get on the scale with an open mind, I am open to expecting the unexpected.

11. It is what it is. So accept it.

If I don't accept the unexpected reflection of a cleared mind, I will probably get back on the scale to see the reflection of my conditioned belief, an attempt to restore the familiar. While using a scale can be a trigger to old thinking, it can, in a moment of wakefulness, reflect the difference between the reinforcement of an old belief and the reflection of a cleared new pathway.

12. I can have my cake and eat it too. This feels scary.

I commit to eating only what I TRULY WANT … not what I THINK I want or have learned I SHOULD want in each moment. This I do while releasing fear thoughts in my colourful hot air balloon or by whatever means is shown to me in the moment.

13. I either TRUST or allow fear (false evidence appearing real) to take me back to the lie that personal ego power can create and sustain change; that this time will be different. Note to self: The only way out of this illusion is through the pain of disillusionment … OUCH!

While I have fallen into the illusion of personal control many times since becoming aware, it's taking less time to realize I've fallen asleep to what I know.

14. Despair helps increase willingness and openness to a new way.

The despair I experience when I've fallen into the illusion eventually serves to wake me up. I see it working in tandem toward longer periods of living a new way … aware of Life living me rather than an egoic *me* thinking itself powerful over Life.

15. I will eventually cease fighting anything or anyone, even my true Nature.

It begins and ends within me has decreased the drama caused by unconscious projection/reflection.

I become trusting of my inner Self/true Nature. Its guidance, when followed, strengthens this relationship above all others. (Religiously speaking, one might say, "God first.")

I believe this can be more difficult for females as we are, by nature, prone to put others before ourselves so that vulnerable dependents may survive.

Sadly, when this happens more than temporarily in adulthood with another adult, both may experience a weakened signal from this inner connection, resulting in relationship failure both inside and out.

16. A paraphrased version of Reinhold Niebuhr's Serenity Prayer: Accept the things I cannot change; Change the things (I think) I can; Wisdom to know (or learn) the difference.

At 44, when newly sober, I thought there was much that sobriety would allow me to change in others. I went from *drunk and in charge* to *sober and in charge*. Now, acceptance of everything I can't change is growing as I learn from the despair of attempting personal power/ control/ manageability.

17. *REAL*ization: That I, as a personal and separate entity, cannot change anything or anyone, even this perceived self.

There is a creative power operating *through* and *as* me. If I listen to it, form and strengthen a relationship with it, *It* can and will do for a perceived me what I cannot do for myself.

If I accept that my rogue ego doesn't have this power, then I can let go of credit for weight loss and blame for weight gain.

It then follows that, if other egos don't have this power either, I can no longer blame them or cart around the heavy resentment and self-pity that fuelled my misuse of food and alcohol.

18. Only my thinking obscures awareness of Creation creating and extending itself.

Only my conditioned mind, which perceives me as an endangered and separate self, can stand in the way of my experiencing the real power running through me like the life-sustaining sap of a tree. There is no tree without sap. Likewise, there is no *me* without this creative energy which I have been largely unaware of and have felt egoically disconnected from even though that disconnection is not possible.

19. TRUST that everything is exactly as it is supposed to be.

When open to this larger Life identity, I feel safely connected to ALL that is. Personal fear subsides as this larger Life connection is *REAL*ized.

20. Everything is fine.

My adult son was recently in a grocery store *trying* to make a rather simple decision when twin girls came riding by in their mother's shopping cart. They were chanting, "Everything is fine … everything is fine … everything is fine." He *got over himself.*

Step two of the Twelve Steps states, "Came to believe that a Power greater than ourselves could restore us to sanity." (P. 59 *Alcoholics Anonymous*, 3rd edition)

In non-religious terms, I believe my son's experience demonstrates the difference between the temporary insanity of the egoic mind *trying* to figure things out … to have a big think … and the sane awareness of Life's Powerful Tapestry.

To access sanity with weight, I believe I have to become willing to recognize and let go of the insanity of the egoic mind while allowing for this larger connection to inform and do for me what I, lost in my own partial mind, am powerless to do.

A big man wearing a Stetson and smoking a cigar once came up to me at a Twelve-step meeting after hearing me share from the egoic mind, and said, "Remember, whenever you're thinking, you're behind enemy lines."

Addiction: Primary, Symptomatic, Self-inflicted, or Pathway?

There has been considerable controversy over whether addiction is primary or symptomatic.

Addiction has been referred to as an allergy, a chemical imbalance, and a mental health issue.

As recently as 2004, I overheard several mental health providers attending Dr. Durand Jacobs' conference on trauma and addictions say they had previously believed addiction to be self-inflicted.

Some mental health practitioners lack understanding of addictions, experience repeated failure, and conclude wilful self-infliction. "The Doctor's Opinion" in *Alcoholics Anonymous* (AA) 3rd ed., page xxvii: "Many types do not respond to the ordinary psychological approach."

"The Doctor's Opinion", page xxiv, in the AA, 3rd ed. text, refers to the alcoholic's abnormal reaction to alcohol as an allergy that creates obsession of the mind and produces craving in the body. Chemical imbalance?

Also from "The Doctor's Opinion", page xxvii: "… unless this person can experience an entire psychic change there is very little hope of his recovery" and "that something more than human power is needed to produce the essential psychic change."

The AA text, page 64, states, "Our liquor was but a symptom. So we had to get down to causes and conditions."

While the medical model works on biology and public mental health services work with the mind, traditional addictions counsellors acknowledge the spiritual/psychic/inner workings of the client and encourage group support work. Twelve-step meetings offer an environment that can accelerate attachment repair while mirroring defenses and projections.

I have found both personally and professionally that high numbers of those suffering from addiction have been sexually or otherwise abused or neglected in childhood by those unable to love and protect them or by those allowed close to the family.

In 2004, I attended *The Overarching Theory of Addiction* presented by Dr. Durand Jacobs of Loma Linda University. He proposed treatment for the unprocessed childhood trauma underlying addiction saying that without this, one is only treating the branches of the tree while ignoring the trunk and roots. The sufferer might gain four to five years of symptom relief but ultimately, the unprocessed trauma will rise to the surface and act out repeatedly while signalling a need for acknowledgement and release.

I wondered about cancer and weight loss maintenance in terms of a similar timeframe regarding symptom relief.

Addiction is not self-inflicted!

Above my computer is an obituary with a picture of a male in his 40s. He recently completed a suicide after enduring a life of pain caused by two male predators who sexually abused him in early childhood. I feel angry and sad that he has died after heroically trying all his life to mitigate the emotional dysregulation caused by these traumatic experiences.

He, like me and many others suffering this kind of pain, tried various chemical solutions, counselling, treatment programs, and Twelve-step Programs. Psychiatric admissions are common as well, especially for females.

An early *interpersonal trauma* experience of *power over* can create a template for heightened tolerance of unacceptable verbal, emotional, physical, and sexual abuse in an adult relationship.

Dr. Durand Jacobs encouraged us, as therapists, to look at chronic anxiety, chronic depression, and chronic myofascial pain as possible indicators of undisclosed childhood trauma such as sexual abuse, imploring us to be ethically responsible and ask the uncomfortable questions which hadn't likely been asked even with previous psychiatric admissions.

That had been my experience. I had seen a psychologist and a psychiatrist, had entered a twenty-eight day residential treatment program for alcoholism, and had a psychiatric admission following the traumatic loss of both parents in an automobile accident twenty-one months after the end of my 18-year marriage and had never been asked.

In 1984, I wasn't even asked to talk about the trauma that triggered my psychiatric admission. I say this with a bit of an edge and an acknowledgement of personal bias as I believe I have survived thus far in spite of the ignorance I encountered while trying to heal from both trauma and addiction. This only child, already admitting to alcoholism, spent two weeks in a psychiatric ward without reference to the current trauma, was diagnosed manic depressive, and prescribed lithium.

Early into my first year of abstinence from alcohol, I went for a recommended check up with a physician who said, "It must be hard for you not to drink in this hot and muggy weather." I never went back. That one comment showed me she had no understanding of alcoholism. It isn't about thirst!

It is vitally important for the person recovering from addiction to understand the difference between psychiatry and psychology when reaching out for professional help. Psychiatry is part of the medical model which seeks to diagnose *what's wrong with you* and has the power to prescribe medication to a person prone to or recovering from self-medicating; psychology enquires into *what happened to you* that you present these symptoms of internal pain.

During my thirteen years working in private practice with trauma and addictions, I witnessed many cases of over-prescribed medication in women who had been sexually abused in childhood, often three to five anti-psychotic and other mind-numbing drugs.

One woman, who hadn't, to my knowledge, experienced sexual abuse, woke up to having lost fifteen years of her life to over-prescribed medication. When she found her voice, she was angry; boy, was she angry! A female cannot feel empowered without reconnecting to her anger, which has been stifled through societal conditioning and/or medication. And, she is often the one most afraid of her own anger. *Don't forget; you'll end up unlovable and alone.*

I never encountered a case of current sexual abuse that didn't have a history of similar abuse dating back to childhood; likewise, I never encountered a case of current domestic maltreatment that didn't have an historical antecedent.

If the original trauma is simply medicated and left unacknowledged and unprocessed, it has been my experience, it will be re-enacted again and again in an effort to be made known and healed.

Symptoms of untreated trauma are: chronic depression, chronic anxiety, drug and alcohol abuse, dissociation, and somatization. Self-destructive behaviour can be a re-enactment of historical trauma.

Hopefully, these connections can help some to overcome shame and motivate healing.

How is it that Trauma didn't get addressed?

Trauma is not addressed in short term treatment facilities as the primary focus is to curtail the acting out behaviour of substance abuse which poses an immediate and real threat to life and health.

Likewise, most aftercare Mental Health Services treat symptoms: substance abuse management, suicidal ideation, anxiety, and depression.

Eating disorders are considered a medical issue.

Problem Gambling is not called an addiction because it produces lucrative government revenues. A small portion of these revenues is then doled out to non-profit organizations, some of which are trying to address the higher rate of murder-suicides found with this particular addiction.

Process addictions such as internet, relationship, *love*, and pornography are not generally acknowledged for publically-funded treatment. Few *fee-for-service professionals* specialize in this field because the nature of addiction makes it unlikely the client will have finances for treatment.

At age 73, I can honestly say I have needed ALL these services.

I showed up, got an education, entered an alcohol treatment centre, spent two weeks on a psychiatric ward, attended Twelve-step meetings, and attended counselling sessions; none of it got to the root of what was going on with my unmanageable life.

My Unmanageable Life

Step one on page 59 of the *Alcoholics Anonymous* text, 3rd ed., gave me the *name* I needed to describe my life in 1988. It stated, "We admitted we were powerless over alcohol" (Could apply to any substance, person, place, thing, situation, my own ego/self-image) "and our lives had become *unmanageable*".

Although I never entered a gambling establishment, my high risk behaviour in *love* relationships cost me my entire financial inheritance and left me temporarily homeless at age 57.

A psychiatric admission following the deaths of both parents didn't give the name *trauma* to the obvious.

When my marriage ended and my parents died, I went to see a psychologist at a publicly-funded mental health facility.

After a session or two, I told him I needed a psychiatrist because I felt as though I were on a roller coaster ride and needed the carnival attendant to pull the lever that stops the ride. A referral was made.

I heard myself admit for the first time aloud to the psychiatrist that I was an alcoholic.

The psychiatrist appeared to dispute this, saying he thought I was manic depressive, that alcohol use would even out once I received proper treatment.

I remember feeling much relieved to hear this since alcohol was the only thing that helped.

He immediately called the hospital to have me admitted.

It wasn't until I found myself walking down a hospital hallway with the word *Psychiatric* appearing above the double doors I was about to enter that reality hit me, hard.

I was medicated with halcyon and put into a room with a door locked from the outside for the first night.

While I was a patient there for two weeks, no one talked to me about my parents' deaths on the front page of the local paper except for a nurse who lived in the same neighbourhood as my parents.

She said it must have been awful for me and then went to a circular file holder, took out a file, and made a brief note.

That was the end of that.

I was *pin-cushioned* with needles to check lithium levels as it was determined I was suffering from manic depression, now known as bipolar disease.

While in the Psych Ward, besides attending several craft classes, I recall wishing I could help two young female patients with eating disorders. They sat each day with a nurse at a small table in the common area while the nurse encouraged them to eat what was on their plates.

It appeared painful for all three.

When the psychiatrist gave me the prescription for lithium, I nervously laughed saying, "What I really need is a prescription for hugs."

I asked only one question. "Can I drink while taking this?" My recollection is I was told, "In moderation."

I called a former teaching colleague with the request she book us a vacation somewhere warm as I was getting out.

Of course, I continued to drink alcoholically while taking lithium, experienced diarrhea and quit the medication. This was in 1984 and I didn't enter treatment for alcohol dependency until 1988.

Understanding and Acceptance through Personal and Professional Work

A Marriage of Matched Trauma History: Fusion and Rage

After much personal and professional work, I came to understand that my former husband and I had been two wounded people who lacked the modeling and skills necessary to have a nurturing, mutually supportive relationship.

My husband had been raised in his early years by a grandmother in an American town where she witnessed him walking to school alone, apart from other children.

At age eleven, he was sent to a residential school run by Catholic priests.

His parents said they did this so he would receive a better education than municipally-funded teachers could offer. My husband experienced abandonment, lifelong resentment, and unmanageable pain, which he acted out.

While living in residence, he experienced sexual abuse when a priest touched him in a suggestive manner. My husband tapped into an identification with power in order to protect his more vulnerable brother when he was sent there as well.

Each of us had experienced a sexual abuse of power; his conscious, mine unconscious.

This experience can create a subconscious dynamic of identification with either *victim powerlessness* or *perpetrator power over*. Possibly due to age, gender, and circumstance, I had identified with the former; he, the latter.

I had felt magnetically drawn to him as if by a force of nature. Our trauma history fit like the lid on a pot.

A male friend on the university swim team had warned me; he had picked up on a sexually-predatory nature in my future husband. Most of the young women at university found this unnamed element attractive.

Only after the marriage ended did a few of my former high school students, a friend, a babysitter and a teaching colleague confirm the merit of the earlier warning.

Whether seen as an ill-fated romance or judged as an inability to take responsibility for my choices, I believe the relationship between my husband and me, presented a mirror to each other's wounds we didn't know needed healing.

I would come to further understand my husband's pain when, at age 57, I opened my private practice as a registered clinical counsellor working with trauma and addictions.

Seventy percent of my clients were First Nations people in their 60s and older, many male, who had suffered physical and sexual abuse while they were children at Indian Residential Schools.

As children ripped away from their families, they were often told their parents didn't want them, didn't love them anymore.

They experienced abandonment, powerlessness, anxiety, and depression.

"Even the birds stopped singing," said an elder describing his village from which the children had been taken.

Anger and rage came later for some when they felt safe enough to express it.

Some re-enacted their abusive experience as either victim or perpetrator, drowning the pain and shame of it all with alcohol.

Their unacknowledged and untreated pain compounded when it was passed on to their children as verbal, emotional, physical, or sexual abuse.

My husband's rage-aholism made sense; it wasn't about me.

I gained a deeper understanding of my own tumultuous marriage through having been given the privilege and honour of working with these First Nations people for 13 years.

Roots of Fusion (Codependency)

Easily influenced when in a relationship with another, I tend to lose my centre and the *ship* in relationship goes down.

The root of co-dependency begins in a child's experience with its parents: "In order for me to be in a relationship with you, someone has to go away or die to what they think and feel ... to their own experience of reality." Who dies to who they are, to whom they are becoming? The child.

Remember the mascara incident? My father's letter delivered to my bedroom? From that, I learned, *I exist to reflect the pain another refuses to acknowledge* rather than as a separate *me*, a dramatic, expressive teen. It's called fusion, enmeshment, a template that makes a relationship of equality between two individuals impossible.

This fusion makes it difficult to distinguish boundaries between where one person ends and another begins, between what others say you are, and how you see yourself.

Any original relationship template can repeat itself throughout adulthood. While some may call it people-pleasing, it can point to an inability to maintain boundaries around an evolving selfhood while in a relationship.

This type of pain and confusion fuelled a need to seek a more secure connection within myself. I wore out two copies of *The Language of Letting Go* by Melody Beattie, simple daily readings that helped me recognize and heal from this fusion known as codependency.

Personality Assessment: Help to Understand and Accept Self and Others

As an introvert, I have mistakenly thought myself to be shy, under-socialized, antisocial, and somehow flawed. I am simply a private person, an INFP according to the Myers Briggs personality type. Because there are fewer of this type, self-awareness and acceptance through social mirroring is less likely.

A simple 70-question assessment can be found in *Please Understand Me II: Temperament, Character, Intelligence* by David Keirsey. This personality-type assessment can enhance self-awareness and help clarify or affirm career and relationship choices.

While I was teaching pre-combat psychology to the military at Camp Gagetown in Oromocto in 2000, I asked the class to assess if I were introvert or extrovert. A major replied, "I think you're an introvert in an extrovert role."

While teaching that class at age 56, I scored evenly on introvert/extrovert; as a Bachelor of Education (B.Ed.) student in my early 30s, I had scored more decidedly introvert on the original Myers Briggs.

Learning while Teaching

A Lieutenant Colonel in my Group Dynamics class exclaimed, "I often wondered why my daughter looks outside herself for validation of who she is; my son doesn't." His spontaneous pronouncement took me by surprise; in that moment, I got this gender difference too.

This *looking outside oneself* is necessary when it pertains to babies and other dependents in the female's care; not so much, when she needs to strengthen an inner connection that may have been damaged or severed by childhood trauma.

For females, like me, who haven't been adequately socialized, there is good news.

An Upside to Having Been Under Socialized

The inside jacket of *Women Who Run With the Wolves: Myths and Stories of the Wild Woman Archetype* by Clarissa Pinkola Estés, Ph.D. describes Wild Woman as *an endangered species.*

"Though the gifts of wildish nature come to us at birth, society's attempt to 'civilize' us into rigid roles has plundered this treasure, and muffled the deep, life-giving messages of our own souls. Without Wild Woman, we become over-domesticated, fearful, uncreative, trapped."

In Chapter 8, *Self Preservation: Identifying Leg Traps, Cages, and Poisoned Bait,* she writes of loss, addiction, and healing injured instincts through the story of *The Red Shoes.*

So taken by the symbolism of all her stories, in the nineties I participated in and later facilitated a women's group based on this book, complete with a background tape of wolf calls.

In support of a choice to remain single, I learned some lone wolves, upon hearing the call of a pack signalling an opening, choose not to join.

Nature(al) Self-regulation: Water, Nature, Animals … and more

Many trauma survivors find living between the lines difficult due to internal physical and emotional dysregulation. Those who have not experienced *interpersonal trauma* tend to self-regulate through connection with others.

I can still get dysregulated, physically uncomfortable, and emotionally anxious around people. When this happens, I tend to fill the air with words and forget to invite others' opinions; I experience a swirling up and spiralling out of my physical centre, leaving me fragmented and ungrounded. It usually takes a couple of hours following a long phone conversation for me to be present to what's happening in a program on TV.

What can I do?

Any of the five senses will take me out of my *replaying mind* and into the present.

In the shower, I notice the smell of shampoo, the texture of liquid, the temperature of water, and I breathe deeply and feel it.

Later in the day, I feel the water running over my hand in the kitchen sink, look at the trees through the glass, notice if the wind moves them or not, and open the window to sniff air currents as a dog does.

Having protected myself from uncomfortable body sensations and emotions through shallow breathing, I've noticed my breathing change to a deeper, calmer place the moment I'm about to enter one of nature's many trails. This then reopens a connection to my true Nature, which has also been curtailed by my shallow breathing.

Animals, both domestic and wild, have always shown me how to *be where my feet are*. The moment I make eye contact with a deer during my walks or notice a sleeping kitty, I forget *me* and the overthinking that causes muscle tension.

On *being where my feet are*, I have found I can slow a racing mind by slowing my physical pace.

I have been taught that another way out of the mind locked on itself is to think of someone else and how I might help with a smile, a call, a visit, or a question of how they are doing.

The movie *Groundhog Day* portrays the mind singularly focussed on *What can I get?* After many attempts *to get*, the main character asks a different question: What can I do for *you* today?

Caution to my female self: The last one, involving people, can reactivate my co-dependency if I'm not grounded. It can also provide me with a distraction when I'm getting too close to a painful memory that's about to be revealed.

My Eating Disorder; a Work in Progress

Lifting the veil of illusion: A horizontal relationship between cause and effect is being replaced by the *REAL*ization of a vertical source of effects.

I used to fight with everything, trying too hard to impose my will. Only when alcoholism broke this willpower, was I willing to listen to another way. One day, I was fighting with my lawnmower. A reasoning mind would say I had flooded it through my many attempts to start it, but I already knew that; I was a great thinker who thought myself right into alcoholism.

As part of my recovery, it was suggested I back off from obstacles, breathe, listen, and follow a better guidance system that would tell me either *yes*, *no*, or *wait*. The minute I completely let go of conquering the lawnmower, I got a tiny inkling to continue mowing rather than put it away. The lawnmower started on the first try and ran so smoothly over the rough terrain that it was a noticeably different experience. When I returned it to the shed, I was given the insight that my former anger had caused it to choke up; I let go of its horizontal bar with a smile.

As the former horizontal cause of effects theory becomes undone on a daily basis, the computer serves as a great example of how my great thinking mind is not really in charge. Something I do one day appears to work. I feel like a winner, rather smug. Another day, I do exactly the same thing expecting the same outcome, but NO, it doesn't work!

Attempting to manage my weight over 57 years has finally shown me the same principle: the ego mind's powerlessness. I'd join a program and it would appear to work until … OH NO … it doesn't. The same effort put forth would fail to get the expected outcome; in fact, my weight would go in the opposite direction while I felt like a bystander, watching it happen.

Many temporary illusions of success have been followed by ever deepening bottoms.

This repetitive bottoming brought me to a path described in *What My Eating Disorder is Revealing*.

If I can accept that I don't get to put on the brakes or take off the brakes, I can say, "Good-bye to both the temporary pride of weight loss and the shame-filled guilt of weight gain."

PART III

WHAT HAPPENED

From Bottoms to Gateway

Prior to my sobering up in 1988, I wasn't fully aware or appreciative of *flukes, coincidences, serendipities*: meeting my husband in 1962; the baby sitter and big city doctor saving my life in 1975; the inner prompting to look at a telephone bill that ended the marriage in 1982; the ensuing twenty-one months my sons and I got to live in the same city with my parents before they were killed; the 1981 letter given to my father two weeks before his death in 1984.

Sober, I began to notice what showed up and how I fit into it all. It began with the pilot light discovery in 1988 while in treatment for alcoholism, followed by the flashback foreshadowing early sexual abuse.

The 1989 reading of Dr. Bernie S. Siegel's *Love, Medicine and Miracles* created awareness of a link between cancer and the discordant relationship between my mind and body.

My attendance at Siegel's weekend conference in Toronto taught me simple check-ins I could do to renew a relationship with mySelf.

I have gained through the pain of so many *bottoms*. Trauma and the repetitious pain of addictions brought me to a doorway.

While I haven't read the *Harry Potter* series, I can imagine a Platform numbered 9 3/4 at King's Cross Station, visible only under certain conditions.

In order to pass through my invisible doorway, I had to be willing to let go of old ways of thinking, to allow life to unfold until the uncommon sense of intuition and inspiration became my new common sense.

On the other side, I became more awake to serendipitous happenings and to dreams unfolding.

The number four came to light on my shoulders and kept showing up.

I had never paid attention to numbers and knew nothing of numerology, so I hadn't realized my parents' house number 139 reduced to a single digit four (1+3+ 9 =13; 1+3= 4), that a best friend's house number in the same city was also 139, and that a group I would facilitate as a life skills coach in 1990 was number 13.

The co-facilitating employment counsellor told me about the group being number 13 and that numerologically, it reduced to number four even though the non-profit organization didn't overtly acknowledge this.

A decade later, a landlord would give me a door code number 4444 at the same time a work contract gave me a voice mail code number 4444.

The First Nations people I would work with for 13 years would show me further significance of the number four.

I met a woman at Twelve-step meetings who was leaving a 15-year marriage and needed a temporary safe, alcohol-free place for her and her 11-year-old son to stay.

My thinking was, *No way do I give up my privacy*; however, the new way encouraged letting go of old ways of thinking.

Learning to say *Yes* to life, I took them both in.

I soon learned from my deceased mother's sister that I had had a sister who lived only two days and had been given the same first name as this woman.

I had planned a meandering trip across the US with my German Shepherd as in Steinbeck's *Travels With Charlie* .This woman was from British Columbia and planned to return.

In 1990, we took a 21-day *Thelma and Louise* trip across the USA from Fredericton, NB, to Vancouver, BC.

I had also had a dream of living on an island. Being from the East, my limited thinking went to the Bahamas. I had even applied there for a counselling position upon the completion of my M.Ed. in 1989 ... I ended up on Vancouver Island, home of my soul.

The unplanned highlight of the three-week journey was a brief visit to Graceland.

Both of us, recovering alcoholics, felt overwhelmed with grief and gratitude at the enormity of our sobriety in light of Presley having lost his life to addiction.

We sat at a little table outside the gift shop writing postcards until we were able to speak about this. Presley had been shamed by society for exposing his soul. Only his upper body could be shown on the Ed Sullivan TV program because Presley's natural rhythm, moving through his body, was considered unfit for public viewing.

Fortunate enough to have reconnected with our own souls, we felt what this shaming must have cost him.

People asked questions such as, "How could you take a long trip with someone you hardly knew?" or "How did you go about planning such a trip … by miles a day to cover … by pre-determined destinations?"

Without awareness of Lesson 135 in *A Course in Miracles*, we were living *a healed mind does not plan.* We allowed ourselves to be guided by intuition and imagination and the trip felt harmonious. For part of the trip, our destination for the night was decided by a TCBY sign indicating *The Country's Best Yogurt.*

At one point in Colorado, when at a high place with a view, I felt the top of my headrest physically pulled from behind as though by a left-handed child who wanted to peer up between the two front bucket seats and get a better view.

I looked in the rear view mirror, then gradually turned completely around to the luggage packed in the back of the Bronco, sensing I might see something unusual.

I did this out of curiosity, not feeling any fear or threat.

I noticed my passenger was in some kind of private space behind sunglasses and intuitively felt the silence shouldn't be penetrated with words, that words would be too harsh.

It snowed overnight in Aspen, so we celebrated by staying a second night at off-season rates.

The next morning after quiet time, my fellow traveller asked if I recalled having turned completely around in the Bronco two days prior. I had. She went on to say that she had appreciated my not engaging her as she had been shedding tears upon having received a visit from her mother, deceased at 52 from alcoholism. Her mother had been making amends for having left her to raise her siblings on her own.

I asked one question. "Was your mother a small, left handed woman?" She was.

Upon arrival in Vancouver, my new-found friend reunited with her sister and I found a motel. I wanted the Island experience even though it was on the west coast, so I thought up a plan to take a ferry across Discovery Passage to Victoria at the southern tip of Vancouver Island. Victoria would feel similar to Fredericton, a capital city and university town.

I was on my knees bedside looking over a full-page map of the Island when my eyes went to the upper middle section and a place named Campbell River. I shuddered at the name Campbell as it reminded me of a recovering alcoholic I had met before I was willing to acknowledge my own alcoholism.

This is where *The Matrix*, a movie released nine years later, comes in.

After several days' rest at the motel, I went to the lobby and found a receptionist I had not encountered before. While checking out and making conversation, I told him of my planned trip to Victoria. He insisted I take a different ferry to Mid Island. This meant I'd have to then drive south to Victoria.

I found him almost rude, but again, I suspended judgment. I opened my mind to the coincidence of never having seen him at the desk before and his weird insistence.

Signs have to come at me in a two-by-four manner if I have already engaged my thinking mind and a plan has been formed.

Off I went to get in line for the recommended ferry with a forgotten University of New Brunswick sticker on my Bronco's back side window.

While waiting in line, I spotted a woman, coffee in hand, walking to her vehicle farther back in the lineup. I rolled down the window and asked her where I could get a coffee. She started to tell me the ferry offered full service meals and beverages, then paused and said, "Where are you from?"

On her way back to Quadra Island after having attended a conference in Seattle, she explained that Quadra is a Gulf Stream Island between Vancouver Island and the BC mainland. It's another ten-minute ferry crossing from Campbell River to Quadra.

She suggested we meet on the ferry. We did and she offered me a tour of Quadra. She knew the owner of an island motel, closed for the season, and could arrange accommodations for me.

Quadra felt like the number four to me and the name Campbell River resonated, so I followed, suspending the left-brain reasoning mind of my first 44 years of living.

I had heard at my first few Twelve-step meetings, "Your best thinking got you here" right into self-destructive drinking from trying to manage your life. I couldn't argue with that as I warmed the seat of many a hard chair.

Having completed three university degrees, I could have added that my education hadn't done a lot to show me how to live either.

As a last resort, I had become willing to take a high wire journey without a net.

While travelling west with my relatively unknown companion, I had talked about wanting to live in a log cabin.

Because I was now following an inner guidance rather than leading with my reasoning mind, I was open to checking out a log house no longer on the market. It belonged to someone my new Quadra friend knew.

She called the owner, telling her a person named *Lori* was interested in seeing it. The owner's slight reluctance melted and we met. I loved the property and made an offer.

I realized the former judgments of my rational mind would scream, *Irresponsible! Impulsive!* It seems that while taking the property off the market, the owner had intuited that a male named *Laurie* would be purchasing her home when the time was right.

The owner had known it was a done deal before we met. The asking price and purchasing price were agreeable to both. The lawyer I used expressed surprise; he thought this was too easy.

I was staying at a furnished motel with utensils and planning to purchase a home in BC where there's a graduated tax on the amount of the purchase. I sat down and figured that I would need $5000 to settle in with basics.

While I could access that amount by borrowing on investments, before I needed to do that, I received a check in the amount of $5,250 at my newly opened General Delivery mailing address on Quadra Island.

It supposedly found its way through several mailing address changes and originated from an investment my parents had held before their deaths six years prior.

The Bridge of Discernment: Conditioned Thinking and Inner Signals

At six years sober, I told myself *a story* … that I felt lonely … that *the man I am to partner with is about to arrive on the Island.* While feeling acute loneliness that threatened to break my chest open, I also felt a subtle inner nudge to get out on the water in a canoe.

I pressured an acquaintance, who managed a seaside resort, to go out on the water with me. Because she couldn't swim and was deathly afraid to do this, she introduced me to a tall, handsome man, who had newly registered at the resort.

Another subtle message had occurred just before I met this fellow. I was at a Twelve Step Series workshop where we were doing rotational reading of a text. My section fell on a paraphrased version of, *Some of us are meant to remain single to better serve our purpose.*

This resonated within me as lightly prophetic.

Still, conditioned thinking overrode this subtle hint with some rendition of, *Something's missing if you're not in a relationship.*

The person I went canoeing with appeared unlike my former relationship pattern.

What I didn't see was that at 49, I was repeating what I had done at 19 … throwing everything away for a relationship when my true Nature was best suited to a single life.

In Twelve-step meetings, I had heard that some of us needed to replace *Ready, Fire, Aim* with *Ready, Aim, Fire.* Mental health practitioners would likely refer to this as poor impulse control.

I invited him to move in with me within two weeks, we formed a company within six weeks, and I felt no resistance to investing all my money and heart in him as I never had in myself.

Both of us were sober alcoholics from neglectful childhoods.

What happened? How did it end? Well, I went to see a psychiatrist, went on medication, tried walking alone and with others, and tried vegetarian cooking. Nothing worked to change a growing inner unrest I couldn't afford to acknowledge since I was so *all in* in this relationship.

Three years into it and without warning, both he and I heard a voice come through me saying, "I want out of this relationship."

Because I hadn't consciously grasped this *out loud revelation*, when the phone rang, I found myself laughing over something a friend was saying.

The relationship was over.

I felt devastated that my unwillingness to heed the earlier prophetic message had contributed to another's pain. The person, the company, and my inheritance … all were gone.

I felt at peace despite the losses.

A subtle nudge had led me onto the water in a canoe and a voice coming through me had ended the three-year journey.

The Flow Streams *through* my True Nature Again

I needed to move out of the waterfront property we had purchased together as I was finding it too difficult to move on while staying where my feet were. I spotted a duplex for rent by a realtor, but I had no money. I called the number anyway and was told I'd need $900.

One of my banks called saying I had overpaid a credit card by $900 and a bit. Rather than keep it as a credit, they were asking when I'd be in to collect the money.

I wanted to move ASAP and there were tenants living in the duplex. Surely they would need notice. The realtor told me the tenants were willing to be out in three days. I moved in.

In 1999, I was back in New Brunswick where I had a son, daughter-in-law and a second granddaughter. I wanted work but had been away for ten years.

Through a friend, I learned one of the universities was soliciting community members to teach. Translated, this meant the university wanted professional services provided for a stipend.

The day of the university interview, I ended up on the wrong floor.

Along with *nothing happens by mistake*, I had learned to consider the possibility, *I'm not where I am for the reason I think I am.*

While waiting, I read the bulletin board and saw the Royal Military

College (RMC) in Kingston, Ontario, was looking for someone to teach the military at Gagetown.

Through a telephone interview, I was awarded the RMC contract, was well-paid, and found the learning experience to be mutually satisfying.

A Ten Year Bi-Coastal Lifestyle

When the contract was completed, I continued a ten-year bi-coastal lifestyle; in 2000, I returned to BC where my younger son was living.

Once again, looking for work, I interviewed for substitute group facilitator work with women recovering from addictions.

The interviewers hired me for this short-term work and generously gave my name to a non-profit society that provided counselling services to women who had experienced interpersonal trauma.

Because the Society's new-hire backed out of the contract two days before start-up, I got the work that linked trauma and addictions.

While servicing these two contracts, I opened a private counselling practice specializing in trauma and addictions.

The Cat is Back!

A sixteen-pound grey and white cat broke into my downtown counselling office. I hadn't had a cat for seven years due to my bi-coastal, nomadic lifestyle. After overcoming my initial fear he might be a savage cat from the rip rock along the water's edge, I needed to get him out of the office. I was subletting part-time to another counsellor and some clients might have had allergies.

This seemingly stray cat showed me what surrender can look like. He willingly came out from under the office loveseat and sat in the middle of the floor.

I hesitatingly picked him up and took him home to the apartment I was renting. My younger son had moved from Vancouver and was providing personal assistant services to my growing counselling practice.

We took the cat to the SPCA to see if someone was looking for him. They asked that we hold the cat for a week while they checked.

The cat escaped the apartment and found his way back to the office, more than a mile away, five days later. The subletting counsellor called, not pleased, to tell me the cat had jumped on her client's lap. My son and I, carrier in tow, hurried to the office to get the cat.

The week was up and having had no call from the SPCA, the cat was ours!

The landlord had a different idea.

We had to move.

While living in Campbell River in the 90s, I used to drive by a little blue cottage across from the water on Island Highway. It nostalgically reminded me of the post war bungalows in Fredericton.

Most apartment rentals wouldn't allow pets. I noticed an 800 number in the local paper listing a house for rent. I reached the owner who was working a four-year contract in Alberta. He gave me the address and I did a drive by.

It was the little blue cottage available at affordable rent!

My son jokingly told someone that when the landlord did return from Alberta, he'd probably find me on the roof, strapped to the chimney, unwilling to leave the little blue cottage.

The side entry had a whiff of older home smell that I loved. There were apple trees in the long, narrow back yard, so I shared the lane with deer and a black bear. Wooden pane French doors separated the large kitchen from the living room, which looked out over Discovery Passage.

A golden August moon sat on the water as I walked from the kitchen into the living room.

We Bought a House!

Three and a half years in, I began to look for a house we could afford to buy. Not easy on Vancouver Island given my financial constraints. I had had a bankruptcy from having invested everything in that business and last relationship, and I was self-employed.

I went to see a mortgage broker next to my office. Given a pre-approval amount, my son and I drove by a dozen homes listed in the paper. We felt discouraged as we realized we would need fifty thousand above the approved amount if we were to find anything.

One day, between clients, I decided to call a realtor. She suggested a property to which I immediately said *No*. I remembered it as a residential area for young families.

Realizing the *no* was a flag indicating my mind was closed, I called her back with a *yes* and arranged a viewing. I called my son to suggest he drive by, and that I'd meet him there if he felt interested.

My first impression of the cedar board rancher with a full-length front deck was that it would be nice to have thicker posts and no busy railing on the deck, a simpler, cleaner look.

We both knew upon entering that this was the house we wanted even before seeing it all.

There were a few hurdles, which my son and I were grateful for. Each of us had learned that if it was meant to be, it would be ours. We had learned not to force things.

There was a first dibs hold on the house by a couple from Vancouver hoping to retire to the Island. Both the hold offer and the asking price put the house at $12,000 more than our pre-approved amount.

I still liked the little blue cottage, but the landlord was supposedly returning to the Island. I had called him only a couple of times in the three and a half years we rented, and he had returned my calls within 24 hours. This time he didn't.

A week went by, the hold was relinquished and negotiation began. Within 12 hours, a deal was struck with the realtor making up the remaining difference between asking and offering. She was a double agent, so her profit was made.

The Broker said, "Getting this mortgage was almost too easy."

The landlord called. I gave my 30-day notice.

Because money was so tight, I had done my homework regarding expenses I might face. The electric furnace, in working order, was the age of the house: 39 years old. If it had to be replaced, it would cost $1800 and could be put on a credit card.

Oh, No! Foundational Rot!

Five months after moving in, despite having had the house inspected, foundational rot was found at the bedroom end of the house. The inspector had mentioned this in his report as a minor repair we could do ourselves.

After interviewing four contractors, we settled on one. The rot was found to have continued across the front of the house, meaning the deck had to be replaced. The busy railing was gone and six-inch cedar posts replaced the original posts … at a cost of $8,500, which got distributed among three credit cards.

I was too fearful throughout the process to realize I had received the deck and front of the house I had envisioned when I first glimpsed the house.

A couple of weeks after completion, I was having morning coffee in the front room when it hit me. I felt awestruck by the awareness.

Within months, I was offered a Health Canada contract to provide nine days of counselling support in Manitoba at $800 a day plus travel and expenses to be paid out at the federal rate, which meant even more money.

The deck I would never have consciously given myself was paid for!

PART IV

WHAT LIFE IS LIKE NOW

A Turning Point

My *lone wolf self* had to join others in order to heal. This began with an admittance of my alcoholism and a look back over my life.

Continuing *Bottoms* on Addiction to a Personal Dissociated Power

"Addicts, compulsives, and certain spiritual seekers have something surprising in common. They all share an amazing potential to see through the illusion of their own personal power. This potential arises out of their life experience in which they continually find themselves acting on an irresistible urge to do something they know will ultimately bring them problems." Wayne Liquorman, *The Way of Powerlessness*, page 18, Kindle version.

Looking back to *The Story of Me*, I can see how fear began to separate the little girl from her *all is well* connection, and how fear grew into overthinking and obsession. The burdensome belief in her own power over life and death led to her suffering over how she threw the tadpole back.

Then began a partial awakening … *Something more is going on here.*

She felt powerless over the magnetic pull and series of coincidences that led to her future husband. She began to feel grateful certain people were in place to detect cancer, for the inner urging to look at a phone bill that ended the marriage, and the insistence she return for the 1981 letter given to her father two weeks before he died.

Conditioned Thinking and Inner Signals gave her the costly gift of discernment between subtle messages from her true Nature and the solidity of old ways of thinking.

Gateway and *Experiencing the Flow Again* showed her there was a new sheriff in town as a new Source of Power was increasingly witnessed. She began to expect the unexpected and to trust *It* even though it appeared to run counter to what had formerly made sense.

Dr. Carl Jung, Swiss psychiatrist and psychoanalyst, who met with one of the founders of A. A., declared that alcoholism is a spiritual disease requiring healing through deep psychic (inner) change.

I believe that change had begun to happen.

Two Kinds of Energy

I am learning to differentiate energies. The human egoic energy feels forced; I have to dig deep for it, to psyche myself up despite feeling resistance. It involves struggle and strain and when overused, leaves me feeling beaten up by life, road weary.

This is the *I make it happen* kind of energy I believed possible and necessary during the first half of my life … its theme song, Sinatra's *I Did It My Way*.

The other source, first noticed in early recovery at age 44, feels fluid. I found myself driving up Smythe Street in Fredericton, gliding, not noticing rough pavement. Same at the K-Mart cashier line up; I flowed through without feeling physically tired or emotionally weary.

This is the *i allow* kind of energy.

When I notice muscle tension, irritability, and restlessness, I've taken on the human energy of *trying* to have things *other than* the way they actually are. I'm opposing the natural order of things and I'm not at peace.

It's as simple as my non-acceptance of the weather. I will suffer if I don't get on board with *it is what it is (right now)*.

This example also pertains to my self-image, other people, places, situations, all things imaginable. I don't have to like or agree with it; I do have to surrender to *it is what it is* if I want peace within myself. The alternative is: I eat, drink, smoke, shop, exercise, fill in the blank … *at* the situation.

From Rogue Ego to Allowing

Up to age 44 and entering recovery for alcoholism, if I saw a wall or any obstruction in my path, I would take a step back to get a better run at it.

Now, a step back allows me to temporarily remove myself from a tight, narrow view and open to a looser, larger view that may offer a different answer. Zoomed in? … Zoom out to open up.

This Halloween, I felt disappointed when I couldn't find a bag of *Child's Play*. Stepping back for a moment to breathe and call my son about whether to go to yet another store, I was *given to realize* a previous discussion. "Wouldn't it be nice if we could find a bag of just Tootsie rolls instead of the mix?" Guess what was in front of me for the exact same price?

Life Works *For* by Streaming *through* Everything and Everyone

This initial awareness was given to me by a First Nations woman who attended the weekend intensive on Sexual Abuse and Healing in 1989. During a break, she shared a story with a few of us.

She said she was driving home a bit fast when a bird crashed into her windshield. She stopped, got out, and made a roadside tobacco offering to thank the bird for giving its life to make her conscious of her speed.

Back in the car and approaching a bridge she would have arrived at earlier if she hadn't stopped, she came upon a horrific accident.

She said birds have natural radar; that the bird sacrificed its life for her.

Now, decades later, my own experiences show me that Life is working *for* while streaming *through* everything including me.

Trauma and addictions *gave* me the opportunity to provide service to others both personally and professionally.

Likewise, I was *given* the office cat, *The Little Blue Cottage*, the deck, and lots more, along with the difficult stuff.

When one of my two kitties wakes me early from a deep sleep, I get up without hesitation because I now REALize the interconnectivity of Life.

Sure enough, the newspaper has come early this time and would have lain on a wet doormat soaking up the moisture if I hadn't been awakened. Thank you.

Acceptance of What Is

In my former life, if something woke me, I'd have had a *put upon, poor me* attitude.

A slight shift in perspective allows me to see connections. Life experiences have shown me *it is so* even when I don't see it or get it immediately.

In regards to loss, I don't just believe, I have experienced *when one door closes another opens* … or maybe it's a window … *expect the unexpected.*

Losing my inheritance made me face the fear (Face Everything and Recover) of taking my professional life a step further into private practice. Clear boundaries around human interaction allowed me to stay grounded while doing the counselling work I loved.

As to the simultaneous loss of that last relationship at age 53, the following quote says it best:

"Many people … are in ignorance of their true destinies and are striving for things and situations which do not belong to them, and would only bring failure and dissatisfaction if attained". *The Collected Wisdom of Florence Scovel Shinn* (Kindle 60 of 4296)

A Return to Living from the Inside Out

The Secret Garden, in my possession since age seven, showed me the universe is within and reflected outward, creating a world of appearances.

Plato's *Allegory of The Cave* taught me to stop giving power to these appearances. They are shadow effects of my own projections.

Dr. Bernie Siegel and the Twelve Steps taught me to ASK, listen to, and act from inner guidance.

Thoughts I Watch Out for: *Other Than – Should*

I want or even *I think I want other than what is* creates opposition to Life on Life's terms. I begin to feel "restless, irritable, and discontented" (p.xxvi, AA 3rd.ed.), feelings that led to my using in order to numb or escape.

Should is a *No-No!* It says the present *whatever* is not right, creating conflict with Life as is.

At Residential Alcohol Treatment, I asked the therapist, "You mean if I'm reading a book and the laundry is done, I shouldn't *should* myself about getting the laundry out of the dryer?" She said, "No, and don't ever should anyone else either." In either case, you'd be making yourself or them wrong about something, rather than *being* accepting.

We were told we had been *Human Doings* and we needed to become *Human Beings*, finding acceptance of Life on Life's terms.

I Need to Keep It Simple: Spider Analogy

Life flows through the spider creating its world, the web in which it lies around playing dead while food is literally brought in. If a human comes along and destroys its world, Life running through spider, as spider, simply creates another world. The spider, unlike the human, doesn't have to let go of egoic thinking in order to *be* an expression of Life extending Itself.

The spider doesn't *think* as if a separate self whether it should *be* or *do other than* its nature *as* spider.

I don't find it a stretch to imagine that my life, like the spider's, is being created and extended *through … the form of me.*

Daily Signals and Fusion that Heals

Retired, I walk daily at different times, dependent on weather and whim. When I follow an inner inkling, coincidences happen.

One morning at nine, earlier than I often choose to walk, I felt that subtle nudge and off I went. On the sea walk, approaching in the near distance, was a former client, crying with the fear and distress of coming into her own and feeling no longer able to please everyone. I invited her to continue the walk with me, something I couldn't have ethically suggested three years ago.

I love the momentary loss of form when eye-to-eye with a marten or a deer, when noticing the sun on the side of a building, the bright green laurel leaves on a wet winter day, and a *yellow* Peony bush.

What? Yellow?

One thought and I'm back to my thinking mind, popping out of the Present. It's that easy to lose contact with the new kind of fusion that heals.

Where do we go from here?

A lifelong friend, feeling heavy with grief after recently *losing* her sister, quietly asked, "Where do you think we go?"

Who knows? I presently see my true Nature as created and animated by Life Itself.

When no longer animated by this energy, I imagine this form will become formless energy once again.

Living My True Nature

I came across a poem written for me by my mother, H.B. Foster, 65 years ago.

A POEM FOR LORAINE (MINTO)

A gleam of sunshine in a flower

I saw one dark dreary day

My spirits rose, and I felt glad

Much better right away

My gleam of sunshine was a bird

Wings black with body yellow

His song was, well, canary-like

And he was such a jaunty fellow

I think his mission here on earth

Is much like yours and mine

To bring to all, whose life seems dark

A song, and some sunshine.

While I'll always be this only child who doesn't know how to respond to teasing, to show the vulnerability that would allow me to receive, and *to play well with others*, ALL IS WELL when I live my true Nature, which has been to learn and to empower others through sharing.

REFERENCES AND READING SUGGESTIONS

Self Discovery and Healing

An Unknown Woman by Alice Koller

Autobiography in Five Short Chapters by Portia Nelson

In the Realm of Hungry Ghosts by Gabor Maté, MD

Please Understand Me II by David Keirsey

The Courage to Heal by Ellen Bass and Laura Davis

The Language of Letting Go by Melody Beattie

Living the Truth by Keith Ablow (fiction is recommended also)

The Secret Garden by Frances Hodgson Burnett

The Tao of Pooh by Benjamin Hoff

Winnie the Pooh by A. A. Milne

Women Who Run With the Wolves by Clarissa Pinkola Estés, Ph.D

Spiritual Process Work

Alcoholics Anonymous (Judeo Christian language)

A Course in Miracles (Judeo Christian language)

The Collected Wisdom of Florence Scovel Shinn

The Way of Powerlessness by Wayne Liquorman

Professionals on Trauma and Addictions

Dr. Bessel van der Kolk

Dr. Durand Jacobs

Dr. Gabor Maté

Movies

Groundhog Day

The Matrix

The Truman Show

BIOGRAPHY

H. L. Foster is a retired professional counsellor, group facilitator, workshop leader, and teacher.

Lori provided services to private and public sectors on both coasts of Canada, including the Canadian Military in New Brunswick and military families in British Columbia.

Passing It On before Passing On is an offering of the personal and professional experiences she found most valuable.

A nature and animal lover, the mother of two adult sons and two granddaughters, Lori currently lives on Vancouver Island in British Columbia, Canada.

www.ingramcontent.com/pod-product-compliance
Lightning Source LLC
Chambersburg PA
CBHW030825060726

47590CB00004B/1393